SPARTA!

Kylie Burns

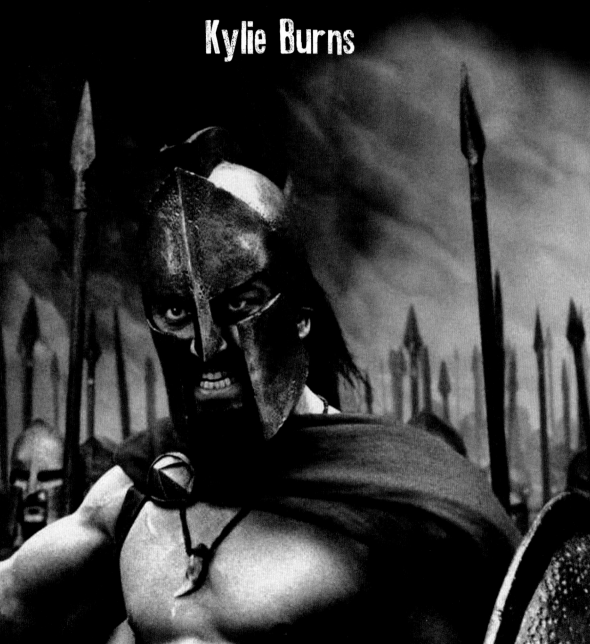

 Crabtree Publishing Company
www.crabtreebooks.com

Crabtree Publishing Company
www.crabtreebooks.com

Author: Kylie Burns
Publishing plan research and development:
  Sean Charlebois, Reagan Miller
  Crabtree Publishing Company
Photo research: Sonya Newland
Editors: Sonya Newland, Kathy Middleton
Proofreader: Crystal Sikkens
Design: Basement68
Cover design: Ken Wright
Production coordinator and prepress technician: Ken Wright
Print coordinator: Katherine Berti

Produced for Crabtree Publishing by
White-Thomson Publishing

Picture Credits:
Alamy: AF Archive: pp. 1, 24–25, 28–29; The Art Gallery Collection: pp. 6–7; North Wind Picture Archives: pp. 12–13, 18–19, 32–33; VPC Travel Photo: p. 16; **Corbis:** National Geographic Society: pp. 8–9, 17, 34–35; Bettmann: pp. 20–21, 30–31; Brooklyn Museum: pp. 22–23; Stefano Bianchetti: pp. 42–43; **Dreamstime:** Heywoody: front cover, pp. 3, 26–27; Getty Images: Massimo Taparelli d'Azeglio: pp. 4–5; DEA/A. Garozzo: p. 44; **Shutterstock:** Panos Karapanagiotis: p. 14; Anastasios71: pp. 15, 45; Topfoto: The Granger Collection: pp. 10–11, 36–37, 40–41; Fine Art Images/Heritage-Images: p. 38; **Wikipedia:** Marie-Lan Nguyen (2011): p. 39.

Library and Archives Canada Cataloguing in Publication

Burns, Kylie
    Sparta! / Kylie Burns.

(Crabtree chrome)
Includes index.
Issued also in electronic formats.
ISBN 978-0-7787-1099-8 (bound).--ISBN 978-0-7787-1105-6 (pbk.)

    1. Sparta (Extinct city)--History, Military--Juvenile literature.
2. Soldiers--Greece--Sparta (Extinct city)--Juvenile literature.
3. Thermopylae, Battle of, Greece, 480 B.C.--Juvenile literature.
I. Title. II. Series: Crabtree chrome

DF261.S8B87 2013   j938'.9   C2013-900273-1

Library of Congress Cataloging-in-Publication Data

CIP available at Library of Congress

Crabtree Publishing Company
www.crabtreebooks.com   1-800-387-7650   Printed in Canada/022013/BF20130114

Published in Canada
Crabtree Publishing
616 Welland Ave.
St. Catharines, ON
L2M 5V6

Published in the United States
Crabtree Publishing
PMB 59051
350 Fifth Avenue, 59th Floor
New York, New York 10118

Published in the United Kingdom
Crabtree Publishing
Maritime House
Basin Road North, Hove
BN41 1WR

Published in Australia
Crabtree Publishing
3 Charles Street
Coburg North
VIC 3058

Contents

Spartan Society

Ready for War

For days, the small Spartan army had been waiting. Now the time had come. Three hundred Spartan warriors stood shoulder to shoulder, ready to do battle. They stared fearlessly at their enemy —more than 100,000 Persian soldiers.

▶ The Spartan army may have been small, but the warriors were ready to fight to the death.

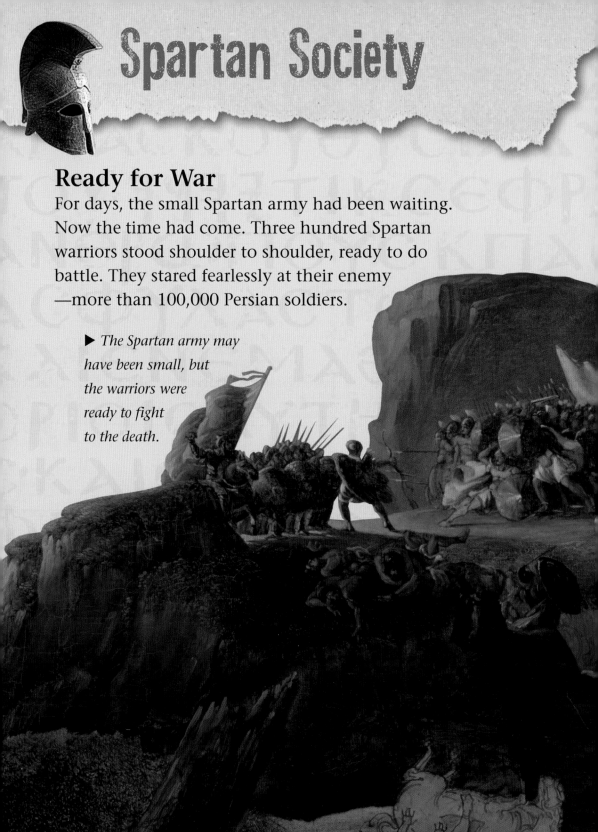

Victory or Death

This huge Persian army had invaded Sparta. If the Persians won this battle, they could **conquer** all of Greece. Spartans would rather die than let that happen. But who were the Spartans, and what made them stand firm in the face of such impossible odds?

The king of Persia was so confident in his army's overwhelming number that he claimed, "Our arrows will block out the Sun." King Leonidas of Sparta boldly replied, "Then we shall have our battle in the shade!"

1250 B.C.E.	Trojan War begins—Sparta vs Troy
700s B.C.E.	New laws turn Sparta into a military state
660 B.C.E.	Slaves revolt against Spartans
490 B.C.E.	Persian Wars begin—all of Greece vs Persia
490 B.C.E.	Battle of Marathon—Athens vs Persia
480 B.C.E.	Battle of Thermopylae—Sparta vs Persia
449 B.C.E.	Persian Wars end—victory for Greece
431 B.C.E.	Peloponnesian War begins—Sparta vs Athens
405 B.C.E.	Battle of Aegospotami—Sparta defeats Athens, ending the Peloponnesian War
371 B.C.E.	Battle of Leuctra—Thebes defeats Sparta

conquer: to take over another country by force

Ancient Sparta

Sparta was located in the southern part of ancient Greece, in an area called the Peloponnese. Around 1000 B.C.E., the Dorians—one of the four main Greek ethnic groups—invaded and settled in Sparta and many other parts of Greece. Sparta became a powerful **city-state**, but for many years its people fought with each other. Sparta was a harsh and lawless society.

▼ *This map shows the city-states of ancient Greece. Sparta was in the region of Laconia in the southeast.*

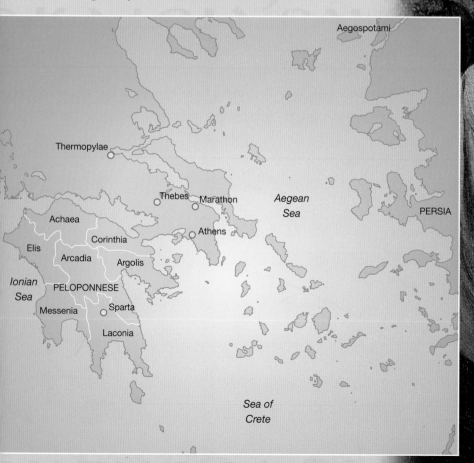

Aegospotami

Thermopylae

Thebes Marathon

Aegean Sea

PERSIA

Achaea

Corinthia

Athens

Elis

Arcadia

Argolis

Ionian Sea

PELOPONNESE

Messenia Sparta

Laconia

Sea of Crete

Sparta's Lawmaker

In the seventh century B.C.E., the Spartan king, Lycurgus, introduced new laws. He divided land equally between all Spartans. He also made laws about training men for war. Lycurgus turned Sparta into a strong military society. Of the many city-states in ancient Greece, Sparta came to produce the toughest soldiers.

"A wall of men, instead of bricks, is best."

Lycurgus, on being asked why he did not build a wall around Sparta to protect it

▲ *Lycurgus was one of the greatest Spartan rulers. His laws were the basis of Spartan society for hundreds of years.*

city-state: an area that had its own rulers and laws

Sparta and Athens

Sparta was not the only strong city-state in ancient Greece. Athens was also extremely powerful. These two states were very different. Athens was a center of art, learning, and **democracy**. Sparta was devoted to training brave, fierce warriors to be ready for battle. Spartans hated democracy. They did not like or trust the Athenians.

▼ *In Athens, boys were taught music, art, and literature.*

Different Lifestyles

People in Athens enjoyed different foods shipped in from other countries. They lived in comfortable family homes. Athenians learned the art of warfare, but they also wrote poetry and performed plays. In contrast, life in Sparta was simple and strict. Spartans were not allowed fancy food or expensive belongings.

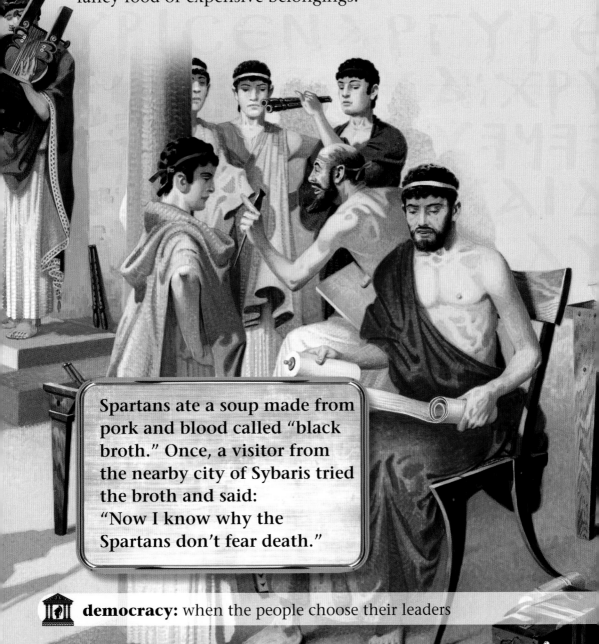

Spartans ate a soup made from pork and blood called "black broth." Once, a visitor from the nearby city of Sybaris tried the broth and said:
"Now I know why the Spartans don't fear death."

democracy: when the people choose their leaders

Spartan Slaves

As Sparta grew more powerful, it began warring with other Greek city-states. In 713 B.C.E., the Spartans invaded Messenia. They wanted to take over the rich farmland in this area. The Spartans won the battle and forced the Messenian people to become their slaves, which they called helots. The helots were the lowest **class** in Sparta. They were often treated cruelly by their masters.

▶ *The Messenians desperately fought to win back their freedom, but they were beaten by the strong Spartan army.*

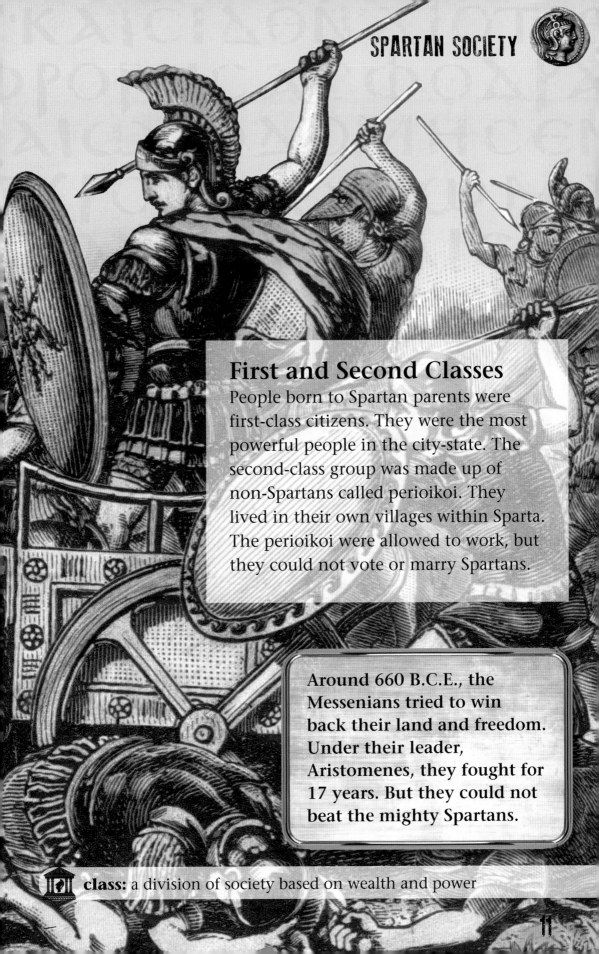

First and Second Classes

People born to Spartan parents were first-class citizens. They were the most powerful people in the city-state. The second-class group was made up of non-Spartans called perioikoi. They lived in their own villages within Sparta. The perioikoi were allowed to work, but they could not vote or marry Spartans.

Around 660 B.C.E., the Messenians tried to win back their land and freedom. Under their leader, Aristomenes, they fought for 17 years. But they could not beat the mighty Spartans.

class: a division of society based on wealth and power

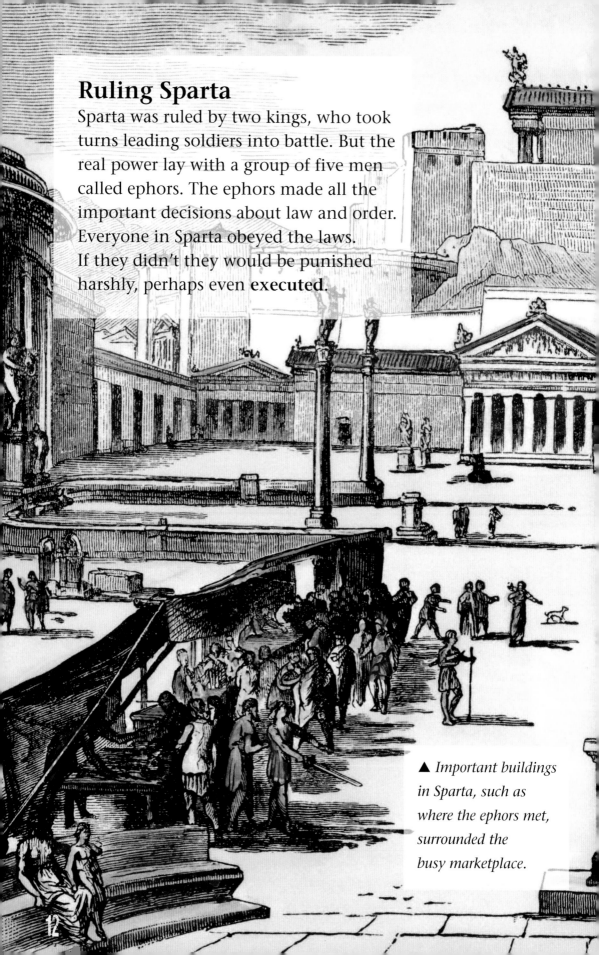

Ruling Sparta

Sparta was ruled by two kings, who took turns leading soldiers into battle. But the real power lay with a group of five men called ephors. The ephors made all the important decisions about law and order. Everyone in Sparta obeyed the laws. If they didn't they would be punished harshly, perhaps even **executed**.

▲ *Important buildings in Sparta, such as where the ephors met, surrounded the busy marketplace.*

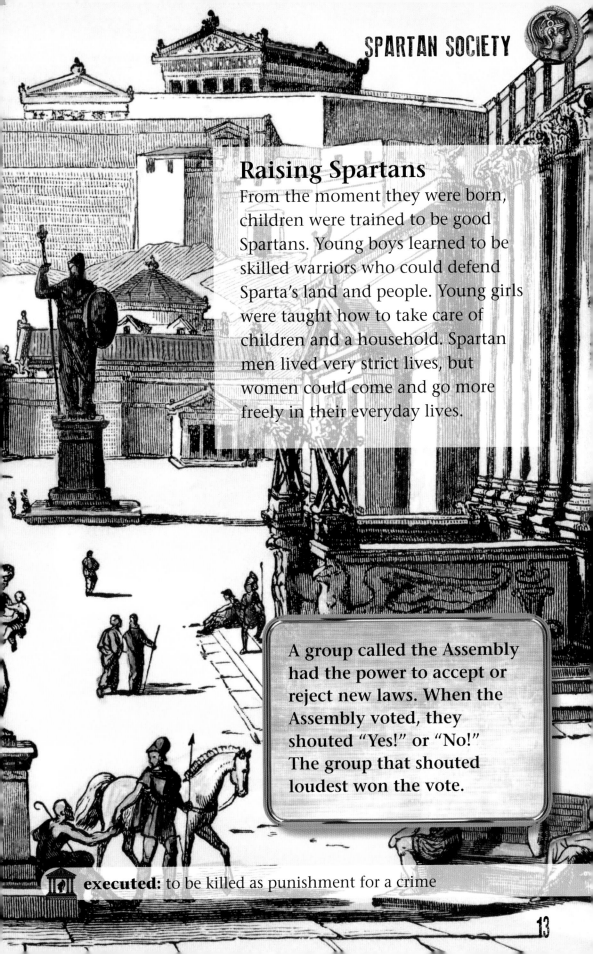

Raising Spartans

From the moment they were born, children were trained to be good Spartans. Young boys learned to be skilled warriors who could defend Sparta's land and people. Young girls were taught how to take care of children and a household. Spartan men lived very strict lives, but women could come and go more freely in their everyday lives.

A group called the Assembly had the power to accept or reject new laws. When the Assembly voted, they shouted "Yes!" or "No!" The group that shouted loudest won the vote.

executed: to be killed as punishment for a crime

A Military Society

After the Messenian helot **revolt**, the Spartans
devoted all their time and effort to building
a stronger army. They forced the helots to farm
their land and care for their animals. This meant
the Spartans could spend their days training
to become even more skillful soldiers.

▼ *Sparta was safely protected by three mountain
ranges: Taygetos, Parnon, and Acadian.*

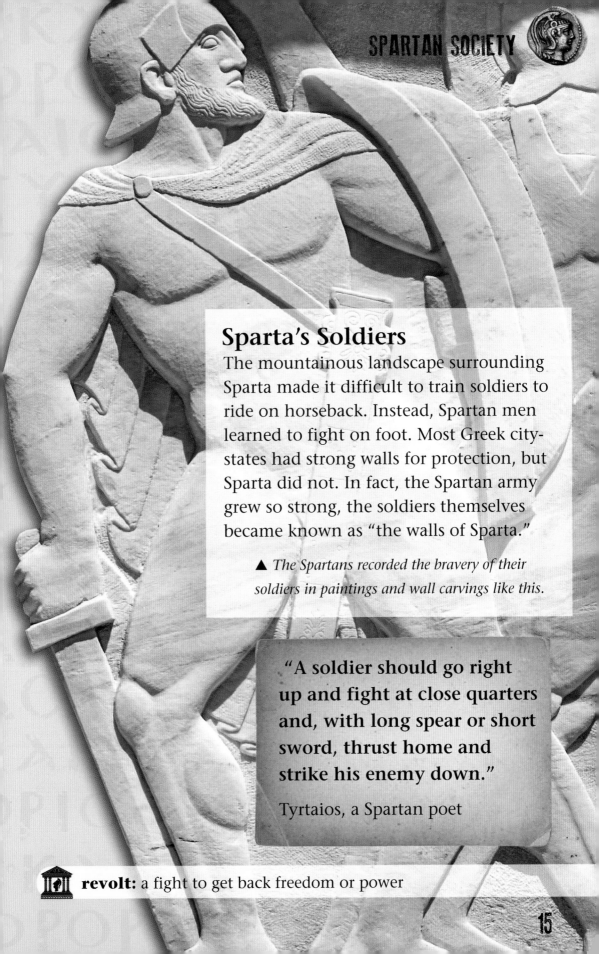

Sparta's Soldiers

The mountainous landscape surrounding Sparta made it difficult to train soldiers to ride on horseback. Instead, Spartan men learned to fight on foot. Most Greek city-states had strong walls for protection, but Sparta did not. In fact, the Spartan army grew so strong, the soldiers themselves became known as "the walls of Sparta."

▲ *The Spartans recorded the bravery of their soldiers in paintings and wall carvings like this.*

"A soldier should go right up and fight at close quarters and, with long spear or short sword, thrust home and strike his enemy down."

Tyrtaios, a Spartan poet

revolt: a fight to get back freedom or power

Growing Up in Sparta

A Boy's Life

In Sparta, learning to be a good soldier was more important than knowing how to read and write. At the age of seven, boys were taken from their families and sent to live in **barracks**. There they were trained in physical fitness. They were treated harshly so they could learn how to handle pain.

▲ *Every year, Spartan boys would take part in an athletics festival called the Gymnopaedia, which means "unarmed youth."*

Stealing to Survive

Boys were encouraged to steal food without being discovered. Spartans believed this was good survival training. If they were caught, they were punished. One story tells of a boy who stole a fox to eat and hid it under his clothes. When the fox chewed into his stomach, the boy didn't show any pain so he wouldn't get caught!

When Spartan babies were born, leaders checked each one for signs of weakness. Unhealthy babies were left on a mountainside to die or tossed over the edge of a cliff.

▲ *When confronted by a Spartan soldier, the boy who had stolen the fox would not confess he was hiding anything, even though he was in great pain.*

barracks: buildings where soldiers live and train

Whipping Contests

When they were teenagers, boys took part in different contests as part of their training. In one contest the boys were struck with whips. They were not allowed to show any pain. This proved that they would be tough soldiers someday. The boys who were still standing after being whipped were the winners.

► *The Dromos was a sports ground in Sparta where boys trained and athletic events were held.*

Cheese Challenge

Another whipping challenge forced the boys to grab wheels of cheese from the altar of the temple of Artemis Orthia. Soldiers lined the path and whipped the boys as they tried to pass by them. The winner was the boy who snatched the most cheese without giving up.

Artemis Orthia was one of the most important religious sites in Sparta. It was in a valley just outside the city. Ancient Spartans went there to **worship** Artemis, the goddess of the hunt and the wilderness.

worship: to show love and respect for gods

Joining the Club

Once they reached the age of 20, Spartan men were elected to belong to clubs called syssitia. Membership meant they were now officially soldiers of Sparta. Each syssitia had about 15 members. These men learned to trust each other with their lives and to support each other in battle.

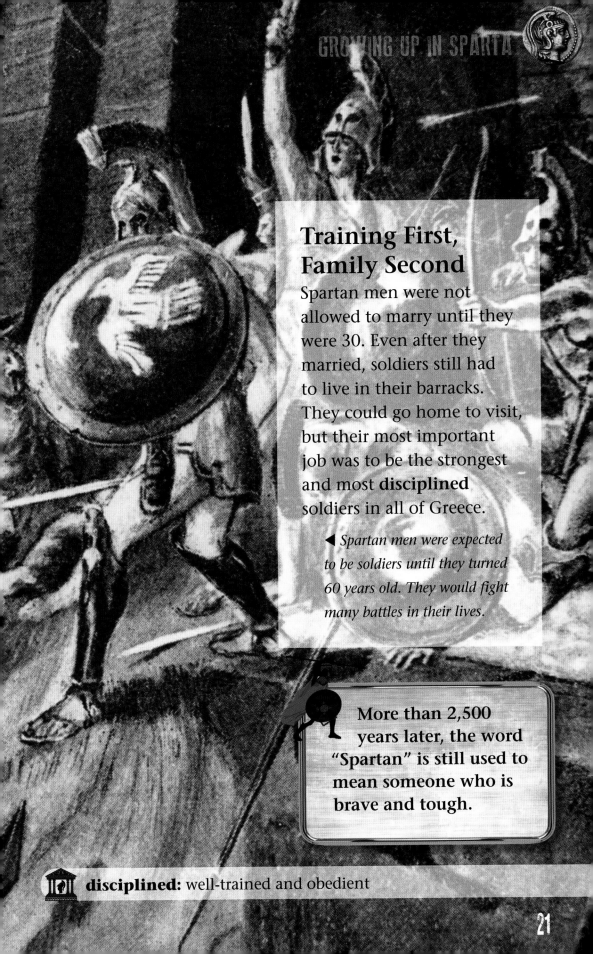

Training First, Family Second

Spartan men were not allowed to marry until they were 30. Even after they married, soldiers still had to live in their barracks. They could go home to visit, but their most important job was to be the strongest and most **disciplined** soldiers in all of Greece.

◄ *Spartan men were expected to be soldiers until they turned 60 years old. They would fight many battles in their lives.*

More than 2,500 years later, the word "Spartan" is still used to mean someone who is brave and tough.

disciplined: well-trained and obedient

Girls in Sparta

Girls were taught how to manage a household and take care of children. Like the boys, they were also expected to be strong and fit. They competed in athletic contests. Spartan girls were not allowed to choose their own husbands. When she was about 18 years old, a girl's father would pick the man she had to marry.

▼ *Spartan girls were trained in gymnastics, music, singing, and dancing.*

A Woman's Duty

A Spartan woman's main role was to give birth to children. Her daily **responsibilities** included taking care of the family and looking after the land, as well as the helots, while her husband was away. Although women did not have the right to vote, they could own land themselves.

"Let the weeping be for cowards, but you child, I bury without a tear. You are my son, and Sparta's too."

A Spartan woman, on hearing that her son had been killed in battle

responsibilities: things that a person is in charge of

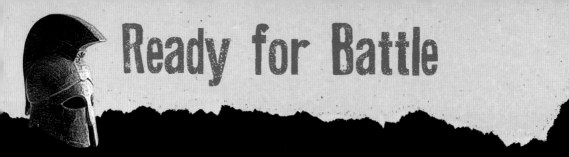

The Hoplites

By the time he was 20, a man was fully trained
and ready to fight for Sparta. Greek soldiers were
called hoplites, after their shield, or *hoplon*.
When a man became a hoplite, his family would
present him with his own shield and body **armor**
to protect him in battle.

▲ *Spartan soldiers wore
bright red cloaks. It is said
that this was to hide the
blood from their wounds.*

Battle Armor

Bronze shin guards protected a hoplite's lower legs from wounds. Metal bands guarded his arms. A metal helmet shielded his head and face from enemy blows. On top of the helmet was a crest of horsehair to make the soldier look tall and fierce. Soldiers also carried a short sword and a long spear.

> Spartan shields often had a symbol on them that looked like an upside-down V. This was the Greek letter L. It stood for "Laconia," the region that Sparta was in.

armor: special clothing worn in battle, often made of metal

No Weakness

Duty and honor were very important to Spartan soldiers. Hoplites never wore shoes. It was considered a sign of weakness if they protected their feet. If a Spartan soldier decided to drop his weapons and run instead of remaining in battle, he brought **disgrace** to his family.

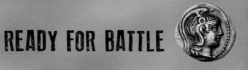
Victory or Death

When a hoplite went off to battle, he was expected to win—or die. Soldiers who returned victorious were greeted as heroes. Those who died in battle were also regarded as heroes. The bodies of those who had been killed were proudly carried home on top of their shields.

◀ *Spartan soldiers feared losing a battle more than they feared death.*

"Come back with your shield, or on it."

Spartan mothers to their sons who were going away to fight

disgrace: shame and embarrassment

Battle Plan

The armies of ancient Greece, including Sparta, marched in a formation, or lineup, called a phalanx. The men formed a wall of overlapping shields and spears. Each row was made up of between eight and 12 hoplites, with several rows behind. The phalanx moved together to the beat of music played on a flute.

▼ *The overlapping shields protected the phalanx as the Spartan soldiers faced their enemies.*

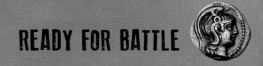

The Power of the Phalanx

During an attack, the phalanx pressed against the enemy soldiers. If the soldiers who marched at the front of the phalanx were wounded or killed, they were replaced by soldiers from behind. A new soldier always took the place of a fallen one. The opposing phalanxes pushed against each other until one broke its formation.

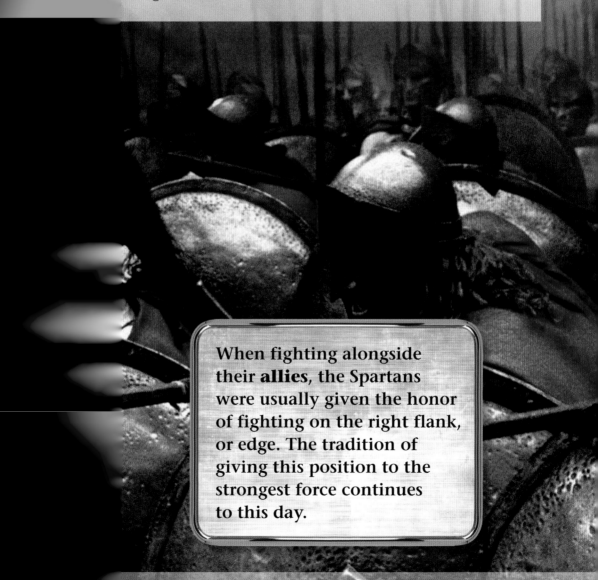

When fighting alongside their **allies**, the Spartans were usually given the honor of fighting on the right flank, or edge. The tradition of giving this position to the strongest force continues to this day.

: people who are on the same side in a war

Sparta at War

The Trojan War

The story of the Trojan War is one of the most famous Greek legends. Around 1250 B.C.E., Prince Paris of Troy **kidnapped** Helen, the beautiful wife of King Menelaus of Sparta. This was a great insult to the proud Spartans. They swore they would destroy the Trojans and bring Helen back to Sparta.

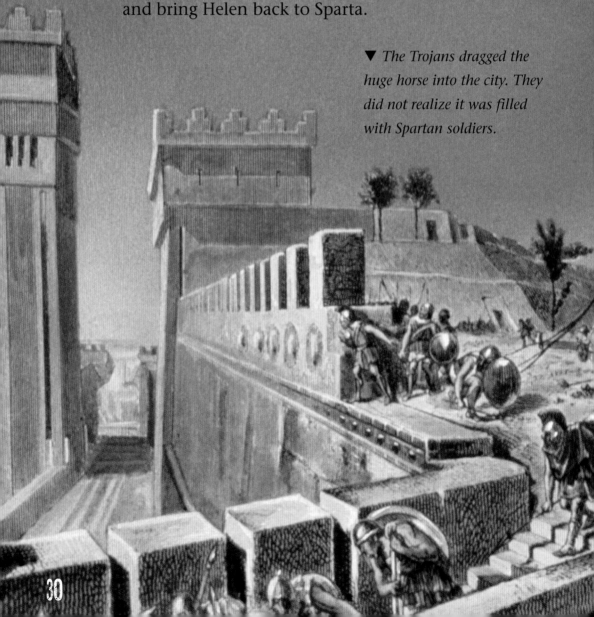

▼ *The Trojans dragged the huge horse into the city. They did not realize it was filled with Spartan soldiers.*

The Gift Horse

After ten long years of fighting, the Spartans came up with a trick to win the war. They pretended to give up and sail away from Troy. They left behind a large wooden horse as a gift for the Trojans. However, many Spartan hoplites were hiding inside. Later that night, the hoplites burst out and took the Trojans by surprise.

The story of the Trojan War was recorded in a poem by Homer, called the *Iliad*, sometime in the eighth century B.C.E. No one knows for sure if it is based on real events or if it is just a myth.

kidnapped: took someone away by force

War with Persia

A new threat came to Greece in 490 B.C.E. The king of a nearby country called Persia (known as Iran today) became angry at the Greeks for giving help to some **rebels** in his lands. For the next 50 years, the Persians tried to conquer all of Greece. Many city-states fell to the Persians. Only Athens and Sparta held out against the invaders.

The Battle of Marathon

The first Persian invasion took place on the plain of Marathon, on the coast near Athens. An army of 10,000 Greek soldiers faced a force of 15,000 Persians. Despite being outnumbered, the Athenian general Miltiades led his men to a great victory. The Persians fled back to their ships.

▼ *The Greeks used a phalanx formation to attack the Persians from the sides and from behind during the Battle of Marathon.*

In legend, a Greek soldier ran 26 miles (41 kilometers) in full armor from the battlefield to Athens to report the victory. Immediately afterward, he fell down dead. Today, the name marathon is given to a running race of the same distance.

rebels: people who fight against the ruler of their country

The Battle of Thermopylae

Ten years later, the Persians tried again. This time they brought a much larger force. More than 100,000 Persians met the Spartan army at Thermopylae, a narrow pass between cliffs and water. When King Leonidas of Sparta realized how badly his army was outnumbered, he knew they had no hope of winning.

▶ *Before the battle began, Leonidas said goodbye to his men and told them: "Have a good breakfast, for tonight we dine in Hades [the afterlife]."*

The 300

Leonidas ordered most of his men to **retreat**. The king stayed behind with just 300 soldiers. The Persians rained down arrows on the hoplites, then advanced to attack in hand-to-hand combat. The brave Spartans held back the Persians for three days, until nearly every one of the 300 Spartans had been killed.

King Xerxes of Persia offered to make the Greeks "Friends of Persia" if they surrendered. He asked the Spartans to lay down their weapons. King Leonidas sent back the message: "Come and take them!"

retreat: when soldiers pull back from a battle

Two Leagues

After the Persian Wars ended, Sparta and Athens signed a peace treaty in 445 B.C.E. But trouble soon began brewing again between the two powerful city-states. Athens formed a group of city-states called the Delian League to protect against invasion by foreign countries. The Spartans feared the Athenians were planning to take control of all the city-states. They formed their own group with other city-states called the Peloponnesian League to fight Athens.

▶ *In 415 B.C.E., Athens' navy was crippled during an attack on Sicily. Athens never fully recovered its strength. This battle proved to be the turning point of the Peloponnesian War.*

Sparta's Peloponnesian League was made up mostly of city-states that held a lot of land in Greece. The members of Athens' Delian League were mostly coastal and island city-states.

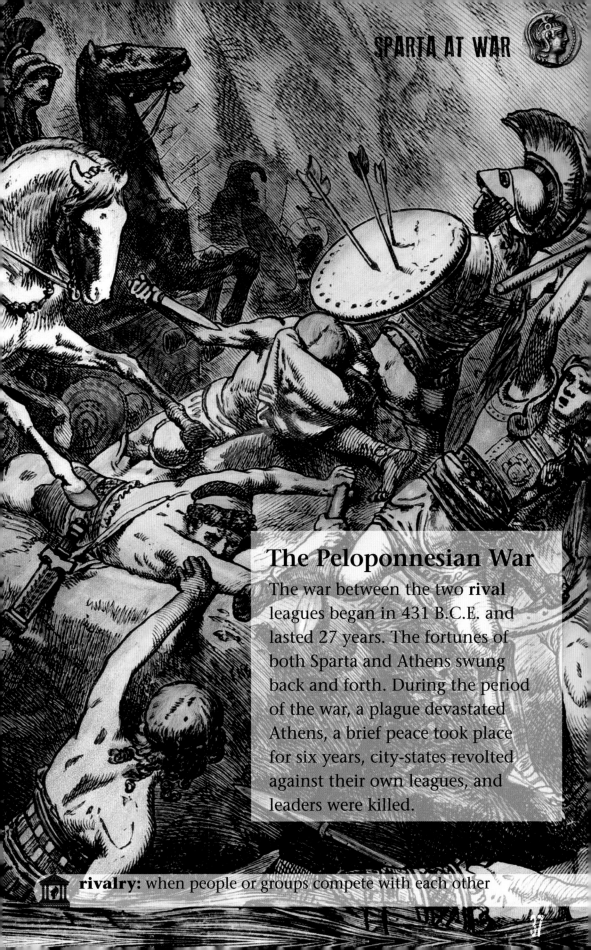

The Peloponnesian War

The war between the two **rival** leagues began in 431 B.C.E. and lasted 27 years. The fortunes of both Sparta and Athens swung back and forth. During the period of the war, a plague devastated Athens, a brief peace took place for six years, city-states revolted against their own leagues, and leaders were killed.

rivalry: when people or groups compete with each other

▲ *Alcibiades grew up in Athens, where*
he studied under the philosopher Socrates.

Traitor!

During the Peloponnesian War, Sparta was
helped by a **traitor** called Alcibiades. Alcibiades
was a citizen of Athens, but he had been charged
with a crime there. To escape arrest, he fled to
Sparta. He told the Spartans that if they protected
him, he would give them information about
Athens to help them in their fight.

Cutting Off Supplies

As a result of the traitor's information, the Spartans invaded the area around Athens known as Decelea. This was where most of Athens' food and other goods came from. The Spartans destroyed their crops and blocked goods from leaving Decelea for Athens. This meant the Athenians had to bring in food by ship so they would not starve to death.

▶ *Alcibiades became an advisor to the Spartans. Later, he fled to Persia after the Spartans became angry with him.*

The Spartans freed 20,000 Athenian slaves who worked in a silver mine in Decelea. Without the slaves, no silver could be mined. This caused Athens to lose a lot of money.

traitor: someone who helps an enemy of their own country

The Battle of Aegospotami

The final battle of the Peloponnesian War took place in 405 B.C.E. It began with a surprise attack. Sparta's army was strong when they attacked by land, but its navy had never been a match for the great Athenian **fleet**. No one in Athens expected the Spartans to attack from the sea. The Athenians were unprepared when Spartan ships attacked at Aegospotami.

▶ *After the great naval battle, Athens was defeated. Sparta became the greatest city-state in Greece.*

Easy Defeat

The Spartan navy was led by the great commander Lysander. He ordered his troops to attack when the Athenian soldiers went ashore to find food. During a mighty battle, the Spartans took 3,000 Athenians prisoner and captured most of their ships. The long war between Sparta and Athens was finally over.

There were 180 Athenian ships at Aegospotami when the Spartans arrived. After the battle, only 20 of them survived and escaped to safety.

fleet: a group of ships

The End of Sparta

Spartan Rule

After the Peloponnesian War, the Spartans took control of Athens. They got rid of Athenian democracy and chose 30 Spartans to run the government their own way. But the situation in Greece was not peaceful for very long. In 395 B.C.E., Athens and some other city-states rebelled against their Spartan rulers. One of these rebel states was Thebes.

The Rebels Win

In 371 B.C.E., Sparta tried to force the rebels to sign a **peace treaty**. When the Thebans refused, the Spartans fought them at the Battle of Leuctra. The Spartans thought they would easily defeat Thebes. But the Thebans had learned some lessons from Sparta's own tactics, especially their phalanx formation. In this last battle, the great Spartans were finally crushed.

◄ *The Spartans lost 4,000 hoplites in their final battle at Leuctra.*

Thebes was a long-time enemy of both Athens and Sparta. During the Persian Wars, the Thebans had even supported the Persians against the two city-states during the final battle at Plataea!

peace treaty: a written agreement to stop fighting

Sparta's Decline

The Spartans had been cruel to the people they conquered, and many city-states rose up against them. They never fully recovered from the defeat at Leuctra. Other states became more powerful, but slowly war weakened even the greatest of these. By 340 B.C.E., much of Greece had been taken over by the country of Macedonia to the north.

▲ *Today, only a few **ruins** remain of the ancient Spartan civilization.*

A Legacy of Inspiration

The lasting legacy of this warrior culture is the Greece we know today. The stand made by Spartan soldiers at Thermopylae inspired the remaining Greeks to band together and fight the invaders. Without Sparta's backbone, Greece might have been conquered by Persia. Greece— and the world— might have looked very different today.

◀ *Statues in modern Sparti remind visitors of the ancient city-state and its great warriors.*

In 1834, King Otto of Greece built a new city called Sparti on the site where Sparta once stood.

ruins: the remains of buildings from ancient times

Learning More

Books

Life in Ancient Greece
by Lynn Peppas
(Crabtree Publishing, 2012)

Hail! Ancient Greeks
by Jen Green
(Crabtree Publishing, 2011)

Ancient Greece
by Anne Pearson
(Dorling Kindersley, 2007)

Websites

www.ancientgreece.co.uk
/menu.html
The British Museum: Ancient Greece

www.history.com/topics/spartans
The History Channel: Sparta

www.sikyon.com/sparta/history
_eg.html
The History of Sparta

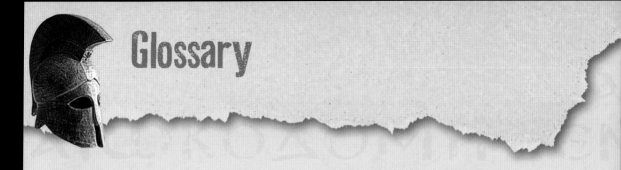

Glossary

allies People who are on the same side in a war

armor Special clothing worn in battle, often made of metal

barracks Buildings where soldiers live and train

city-state An area that had its own rulers and laws

class A division of society based on wealth and power

conquer To take over another country by force

democracy When the people choose their leaders

disciplined Well-trained and obedient

disgrace Shame and embarrassment

executed To be killed as punishment for a crime

fleet A group of ships

kidnapped Took someone away by force

peace treaty A written agreement to stop fighting

rebels People who fight against the ruler of their country

responsibilities Things that a person is in charge of

retreat When soldiers pull back from a battle

revolt A fight to get back freedom or power

rivalry When people or groups compete with each other

ruins The remains of buildings from ancient times

traitor Someone who helps an enemy of their own country

worship To show love and respect for gods

Index

Entries in **bold** refer to pictures